EFFECTIVE SALES MANAGEMENT

Tom Johnson

A FIFTY-MINUTE™ SERIES BOOK

Viva Books Private Limited
New Delhi • Mumbai • Chennai • Kolkata • Bangalore • Hyderabad

First Indian Edition 2004
Reprinted 2005

VIVA BOOKS PRIVATE LIMITED

- 4262/3 Ansari Road, Daryaganj, New Delhi 110 002
  E-mail: viva@vivagroupindia.net
- 215-216 New Apollo Estate, 2nd Floor, Mogra Lane, Andheri (E),
  Mumbai 400 069 E-mail: vivamumbai@vivagroupindia.net
- Jamals Fazal Chambers, 26 Greams Road, Chennai 600 006
  E-mail: vivachennai@vivagroupindia.net
- B-103, Jindal Towers, 21/1A/3 Darga Road, Kolkata 700 017
  E-mail: vivakolkata@vivagroupindia.net
- 7 GF, Sovereign Park Apts., 56-58 K.R. Road, Basavanagudi,
  Bangalore 560 004 E-mail: vivabangalore@vivagroupindia.net
- 101 & 102, First Floor, Mughal Marg Apartments, Narayanaguda,
  Hyderabad 500 029 E-mail: vivahyderabad@vivagroupindia.net

Published by arrangement with

Crisp Publications, Inc.
1200 Hamilton Court,
Menlo Park
CA 94025
USA

Credits:
Editor: Michael G. Crisp
Layout and Composition: Interface Studio
Cover Design: Carol Harris
Artwork: Ralph Mapson

ISBN 81-7649-560-3

Published by Vinod Vasishtha for Viva Books Private Limited, 4262/3 Ansari Road, Daryaganj, New Delhi 110 002 and printed & bound at Raj Press, R-3 Inderpuri, New Delhi-110 012

LEARNING OBJECTIVES FOR:

EFFECTIVE SALES MANAGEMENT

The objectives for *Effective Sales Management* are listed below. They have been developed to guide you, the reader, to the core issues covered in this book.

Objectives

- ❑ **1) To show how to recruit a successful sales team.**
- ❑ **2) To explain sales training.**
- ❑ **3) To explain strategies for motivating salespeople.**
- ❑ **4) To discuss evaluation techniques.**

Assessing Your Progress

In addition to the Learning Objectives, Crisp, Inc. has developed an **assessment** that covers the fundamental information presented in this book. A twenty-five item, multiple choice/true-false questionnaire allows the reader to evaluate his or her comprehension of the subject matter. An answer sheet with a summary matching the questions to the listed objectives is also available. To learn how to obtain a copy of this assessment please call: **1-800-442-7477** and ask to speak with a Customer Service Representative.

ABOUT THE AUTHOR

Tom C. Johnson, a professional speaker and trainer, has worked for a Fortune 100 diversified company as a manager, business development expert and corporate trainer for over fifteen years. During that period, he has led the country in sales and has helped contribute to their worldwide success.

Mr. Johnson is currently on the staff for Northern California Training Council and is an associate of Enlightened Leadership International. He has taught at the University of California, Berkeley Extension, and has spoken to *Inc.* Magazine National Business Conference, being rated as one of their top presenters. A long-time member of the National Speakers' Association and past board member, Tom is also the past President of the Sales and Marketing Executives' Association of the Bay Area. He has achieved degrees from the University of Iowa and the University of Florida.

ABOUT THE SERIES

With over 200 titles in print, the acclaimed Crisp 50-Minute™ series presents self-paced learning at its easiest and best. These comprehensive self-study books for business or personal use are filled with exercises, activities, assessments, and case studies that capture your interest and increase your understanding.

Other Crisp products, based on the 50-Minute books, are available in a variety of learning style formats for both individual and group study, including audio, video, CD-ROM, and computer-based training.

TABLE OF CONTENTS

(Continued on next page)

TABLE OF CONTENTS (Continued)

SECTION

I

What Sales Management Is All About

Who is a Sales Manager

The sales manager holds a crucial job. In addition to building sales, successful sales managers also significantly contribute to the bottom line of their companies.

They hold no magical, supernatural powers. Successful sales managers are simply people who have learned to bring out the best in the people they manage. Successful sales managers know that the needs of the business are best met when the needs of the individuals they manage are met.

According to the great automotive pioneer, Henry Ford, the most valuable person ever to work for him was ''a manager of people'' rather than projects. When it comes to sales, there is no substitute for people management.

SETTING YOUR OBJECTIVES

An important part of being a successful sales manager is setting and meeting objectives. As you read this book, you are encouraged to adopt the following objectives as your own. Those listed below (plus others you may wish to add) will help you in your career. You will learn more about most of them in the pages ahead.

In setting my objectives, I plan to (check those you feel are important):

- ☐ Exploit my intuitive power.
- ☐ Make better decisions.
- ☐ Get maximum production from others.
- ☐ Build a winning attitude on my sales team.
- ☐ Communicate more effectively with my team.
- ☐ Recruit and hire superior people.
- ☐ Motivate and help my sales team develop.
- ☐ Learn other, more specialized techniques that will help me become a professional sales manager.
- ☐ Add your own ________________________________

If you are currently a sales manager, congratulations! It has been estimated that most salespeople experience difficulties learning to become a successful manager. Are you different? Do you have the required mixture of attractiveness, strength and promise, which you can hold together with boundless self-confidence? Do you display conviction about the correctness of your position, even on those frustrating occasions when you find yourself of two minds? If you answered yes to the above, you are well on your way to becoming a successful sales manager.

TEN QUALITIES OF A WINNING SALES MANAGER

The quality of leadership is elusive, at best. It is almost as difficult to define as it is to acquire.

Nevertheless, there are 10 basic qualities that all good sales managers possess. Fortunately, most can be learned. Here they are; check those you possess:

1. **You like people.** We hope you already have this quality! (If you don't, you may as well stop here and return this book for a refund.)

2. **You are well organized.** Organization is the foundation of everything that you do successfully in life.

3. **You have a sense of commitment.** Until one is committed, there is hesitancy and always ineffectiveness.

4. **You have a strong desire for responsibility.** Since you will be judged on results, you know you are responsible for the results of your sales team. And you wouldn't have it any other way.

5. **You are persistent in the pursuit of your goals.** Recognize the value of persistence. Former U.S. President Calvin Coolidge said, "Nothing in the world can take the place of persistence. Talent will not; nothing is more common than unsuccessful men with talent. Genius will not; unrewarded genius is almost a proverb. Education will not; the world is full of educated derelicts. Persistence and determination alone are omnipotent."

CONTINUED

TEN QUALITIES OF A WINNING SALES MANAGER (Continued)

6. You bring out the best in people. The German philosopher Goethe explained this succinctly when he said, ''If I accept you as you are, I will make you worse; however, if I treat you as though you are what you are capable of becoming, I help you become that.''

7. You have tolerance. You understand the art of being human includes allowing people to grow by learning through ''mistakes.'' In reality, you realize there are no ''mistakes''—only steps to mastery.

8. You are flexible. New situations call for different actions over time. You need to know when to direct and control and when to follow and discover.

9. You engage in self-analysis. In a survey, one-third of sales people interviewed were dissatisfied with their manager. Have the guts to accept feedback, and be willing to listen. Along this line, ponder the words of Sigmund Freud: ''Work is man's strongest tie to reality.''

10. You have enthusiasm. All the studies done by the Dale Carnegie organization indicate that this characteristic—enthusiasm—is the number one characteristic for success in life. With it you can do anything; without it, you can do nothing. You won't be alone for very long when you have enthusiasm, because enthusiasm is contagious.

SELF-TEST: BECOMING A SALES MANAGER

Now that you know the qualities of an effective sales manager, take the following personal assessment to see how you measure up to the demands of this job. The answers should make you think seriously about your willingness to invest in a sales-management career. If you measure up, the rewards of sales management are virtually unlimited. Answer the questions honestly.

YES NO

☐ ☐ 1. Do you enjoy your job? (This is a prerequisite for sales management success. You can't fake it.)

☐ ☐ 2. Do you enjoy hard work? People who enjoy the work they're doing find it invigorating and renewing.

☐ ☐ 3. Do you live with integrity? There is no substitute for it. You need to ask yourself constantly, "Could I tell my kids about this?" If the answer is "yes," then it's the right thing to do.

☐ ☐ 4. Do you emphasize results, rather than activity? People are with you for one reason—to make a significant contribution to the company. Are you recognizing the value that they bring to the business?

☐ ☐ 5. Do you exemplify self-discipline? To get others to do their work and lead their lives effectively, you first have to set the example yourself.

☐ ☐ 6. Do you have a broad perspective on life? Seeing the big picture first lets you be a better specialist.

☐ ☐ 7. Are you physically fit? You need a healthy body to have vigorous mental health and activity.

☐ ☐ 8. Do you praise and thank others for a job well done? Recognition is the most powerful force you have available to you as a manager.

☐ ☐ 9. Do you practice candor? Permissiveness and apologetic behavior by managers is never appropriate.

☐ ☐ 10. Are you sensitive to the moods of others? Can you read people well?

If you answered yes to eight or more of the above questions, you have the basics of what it takes to become a successful sales manager. Fewer yes answers suggest you might be happier and more successful in a different job.

WHAT SUCCESSFUL SALES MANAGERS DO

Perhaps more than any other line manager, sales managers are concerned with a range of management activities from planning the future to helping ensure that the required monthly bottom line is delivered.

Luckily, there are some specific actions you can take to keep your organization's revenues strong and the profits healthy. Among the most important are:

1. Create a vision of what you want your sales team to accomplish. If you don't have a target, then no one can follow you.

2. Keep your people aware of their goals. Monitor their performance consistently.

3. Recruit outstanding people. Mistakes in recruiting are unbelievably costly. You need to blend different personalities to get the best results. Outstanding salespeople come in all sizes, shapes and colors and it is your responsibility to get them working together.

4. Create and invest in an outstanding training program. Training is the best way to ensure your people will represent you professionally. It is imperative to start new sales people off on the right foot.

5. Take an advisory role. As a sales manager, you become a coach, a parent, a teacher or a cheerleader—depending on the situation. What you call it isn't important—what is important is that you have to be there when your people need you, and you also have to know them all as individuals.

6. Constantly work on upgrading ***your*** skills. You'll succeed if you have the attitude that you never stop learning.

7. Accept that part of your job will be to terminate poor performers. It is up to you to determine when termination becomes necessary. You must learn to handle this professionally when required and cannot hesitate a moment in this crucial responsibility.

WHAT SUCCESSFUL SALES MANAGERS *DON'T* DO

In sales management, just as in personal selling, it is important to understand not only what to do, but also what not to do. As sales trainer Loren Lasher recently told a conference of sales and marketing executives, ''Where the attention goes, the energy flows.''

With that in mind, following is a list of things to avoid. Check those that you agree are important.

AGREE DISAGREE

☐ ☐ 1. Don't concentrate on negatives. People learn from trial and ''right,'' not trial and error. Instead of telling someone what they did wrong, tell them what you want them to do differently the next time.

☐ ☐ 2. Don't cover up mistakes. Instead, encourage people to report the actual situation. It is essential to know the facts.

☐ ☐ 3. Don't look at mistakes as mistakes but only as opportunities to learn and grow. After all, being human means making mistakes. The biggest winners often make the most mistakes. Good managers know how to convert a mistake into an opportunity.

☐ ☐ 4. Don't allow individuals to perform just well enough to keep their jobs. Good sales managers motivate individual sales representatives by comparing that person's performance in the past to the present. It is completely wrong to compare one person's performance to that of someone else.

☐ ☐ 5. Don't cut people off. Good managers listen. They get agreements on what has been said and understood and probe for clarity. Only when they understand the situation do they decide on a course of action.

☐ ☐ 6. Don't fail to have a plan of action. Effective managers recognize the importance of such things as clear communication, proper goal setting, accountability and follow-up.

As a sales manager, it's important to realize that your authority is based on the power of your personality. Even though you may be in your job because of your knowledge, ability and competence, you can only *stay* where you are by sharing your knowledge with others. This means that to become a professional manager, your relations with other people are paramount.

TIME MANAGEMENT

> "One of the measures of a manager is the ability to distinguish the important from the urgent; to refuse to be tyrannized by the urgent."
>
> —Alec MacKenzie, *The Time Trap*

Time management is more about management than about time. Good time management is about being well organized. People who get things done are usually better organized than those who don't. Following are 15 time management tips for you and your salespeople:

1. Write daily *specific, measurable outcomes* you want to achieve.

2. Every day, review top prospects and determine what can be done to move them closer to a sale.

3. Use a master list of priorities so you can focus on that which provides the biggest payoff.

4. Periodically, ask yourself "Is what I am doing now the most important thing I can be doing at this time?"

5. Establish "place habits." Keep everything in a predetermined place.

6. Create systems for forms, checklists and repetitive tasks.

7. Don't leave tasks unfinished. Complete what you start.

8. Don't do low priority paperwork during "prime calling time."

9. Minimize socializing during business periods.

10. Plan your calls to cut down travel time and commuting.

11. Stop procrastinating. Eliminate indecision. Develop a "do it now" approach.

12. Pre-plan each week and allocate time to perform the necessary functions. Have new hires turn in a weekly plan in advance for your review and critique.

13. At the end of each day, create a carry-over list of items that were not accomplished and work them into an action plan for the next day.

14. Regularly analyze your use of time. Adapt and adjust when required to improve your efficiency and productivity.

15. Put in the necessary hours to accomplish your daily plan.

AM I RIGHT FOR SALES MANAGEMENT?

Why do you want to be a sales manager? If it's for the money alone, you may as well stop right here. Money is important, but to succeed in sales management, you must first and foremost want to make a difference in people's lives and help them become more successful. If that concept sounds right, then chances are good that this job is for you.

Answer the following questions to see if you really want to be a sales manager:

1. Briefly describe your strengths as a manager.

2. How can you use these strengths to bring people to their next level of achievement?

3. How well organized are you? How well do you think you could organize a sales team's efforts?

4. How well do you listen, keep control of a dynamic situation and foster cooperation with others?

5. What other elements of persuasion are at your disposal?

6. How willing are you to take a risk?

7. How much responsibility do you want?

8. How successfully can you adapt to different personalities?

9. Describe your daily work habits. Are you a self-starter? Do you work well without direct supervision?

SELF-ASSESSMENT: SALES MANAGEMENT SKILLS

Carnegie-Mellon University recently interviewed a group of salespeople and reported that 95% of those interviewed said they could be more productive on the job. As a sales manager, your primary job is to make your team more productive.

Take the following simple test to learn how you rate in important sales management skills. If there is an area that needs improvement, a handy reference has been provided to tell you where this topic is covered in this book.

	YES	NO	SECTION
Can you transcend previous levels of accomplishment?	☐	☐	I
Are you driven by compelling internal goals?	☐	☐	I
Can you accept consequences of your actions?	☐	☐	V
Can you recognize how to reward your best performers at all levels?	☐	☐	V
Can you sustain high performance?	☐	☐	IV
Can you recognize and hire the best performers?	☐	☐	II
Do you genuinely like people?	☐	☐	I
Do you remember that criticism brings out the worst in people, while appreciation brings out the best?	☐	☐	IV
Do you respect the differences between you and other people?	☐	☐	III
Do you act enthusiastically even if you don't feel enthusiastic?	☐	☐	III
Do you ask advice from people and allow them to make a contribution?	☐	☐	IV

SECTION

II

Recruiting

Your success will be determined more by the quality of the people you hire than by anything else. It is generally known that 50% of customers leave an account because of the salesperson. In today's environment, you can't afford to make a mistake in hiring—your success (or failure) rests squarely on the shoulders of the people you decide to bring onto your team.

This chapter will give you a comprehensive yet concise view of how to go about finding people to inverview, what to look for when you have them in front of you and how to evaluate them when it's time to make the crucial choice of whom to hire and whom to reject.

The number one criterion for making good hiring decisions is knowing what you want. This chapter will also help you put together your ideal sales team by clarifying what you want in a new hire.

BEGINNING YOUR SEARCH

You start the recruiting process by organizing a planned search. Though you may have to interview several candidates before you find the right person, the good news is that the time invested is worth it. In the end, the right person will not only be the one you want, but also the one that wants you.

How do you find potentially strong candidates? The following three ways work well:

1. **Competitors.** It is very likely there is a person involved in sales that is a strong competitor. Find out who that person is and see if that individual is interested in talking with you about your position.

2. **Advertisements.** This is the most conventional way to hire a new salesperson. Here is a suggestion: Set up a phone screening system and pre-interview candidates on the the phone. If they cannot sell you on their candidacy on the phone, don't bother to arrange an in-person interview.

3. **Search firms or similar agencies.** According to a recent study, one out of four sales positions will be filled using recruiters or ''head hunters'' in the future. A good agency or service will have a clear idea of the capability of candidates. While such services can be expensive, it is not really possible to put a price on finding the best individual for the job. For best results, make sure the search firm clearly understands your needs and your corporate culture.

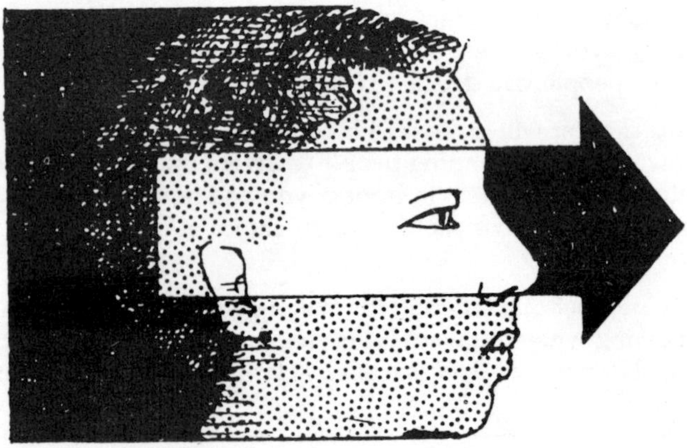

SELECTING YOUR SALES TEAM: EXERCISE

In making hiring decisions, certain attitudes and regular habits keep your successes high. Take the following survey to see how many of the eight questions you can answer "yes." For any question where you answer "no," consider revising your thinking to incorporate some new constructive tendencies.

	YES	NO
1. Do I know how many salespeople I really need?	☐	☐
2. Do I have a game plan to replace a key person during a peak sales season?	☐	☐
3. Do I possess a realistic awareness of the marketplace?	☐	☐
4. Am I constantly looking for good potential candidates? Do I keep a file on them?	☐	☐
5. Do I spend enough time gathering information about strong competitors?	☐	☐
6. Do I constantly meet with potential hires? (Hint: Don't wait until you need people to do screening.)	☐	☐
7. Am I on schedule with my sales goals? Do I need additional resources?	☐	☐
8. Do I enjoy prospecting, interviewing and hiring salespeople? Do I understand that this is the key to success in sales?	☐	☐

CONDUCTING THE INTERVIEW

The hiring interview is not strictly a numbers game. Your people skills are equally important. Your interview should be a free-flowing discussion. Your candidate should be encouraged to open up and talk. Since you have a good idea of the type of person you want, listen hard to determine how your candidate's responses fit the criteria you are looking for.

Asking open-ended questions (those that cannot be answered with a simple yes or no) allows you to find out what motivates candidates and what each wants from the job. Make absolutely sure you understand what the potential employee wants from you as an employer. A good match between their wants and needs and yours will go a long way toward creating a successful employment situation.

Following is a list of Do's and Don'ts that may be helpful.

Do:

1. ...Know what questions you want to ask. Prepare a menu of questions that determines if your candidate has the basic ability, work experience, attitude and motivation to perform successfully.

2. ...Pay close attention to the answers you receive. When you know specifically what you want to achieve, it is easier to recognize the right answers when you hear them.

3. ...Be aware of their first impression. If you felt comfortable and relaxed by their appearance and body language, it is likely your customers will feel the same way.

4. ...Start with broad, introductory questions, and follow up with specific questions. Keep in mind interviewing is a form of communication. You want an exchange of ideas, opinions and feelings between two people.

Do:

5. ...Establish rapport. Initiate "small talk" about the weather, sports, etc. before you lead into your introductory questions. You should keep the format the same for all interviewees. This allows you to compare how each individual handled the situation and should provide you with a consistent evaluation process.

6. ...Give them the ball, and let them run with it. Provide lots of room to show you who they are, whether or not they did homework before the interview and whether they are the person to best meet your needs. Most of all, you allow them to improvise and go with the flow. This will give you a good idea of what they will be like in a live sales situation.

7. ...Be sure to ask questions about their previous job-related experiences, especially focusing on what they feel are their strengths. Make sure you receive an up-to-date list of personal references—including individuals who have firsthand knowledge of their work habits.

8. ...Notice their ability to ask meaningful, thoughtful questions. Good questioning techniques are a major part of any successful salesperson's arsenal.

CONDUCTING THE INTERVIEW (Continued)

Here is a list of don'ts for you:

Don't:

1. ...Be too quick to prejudge. The ability to sell is an aptitude that eludes scientific efforts people have made to measure it. Keep your mind open to the idea that each candidate might be the right person, but do keep first impressions in mind.

2. ...Fail to notice the characteristics that allow people to excel in unique, and perhaps unexpected, ways. Uncover these characteristics by asking candidates to describe their last two years of work in detail. Listen astutely to find out if what they are telling you will fill the key requirements of your job, even if it's in an unexpected or unorthodox way.

3. ...Rely on tests. Tests can be poor indicators of sales aptitude. Often tests tend to measure interests instead of abilities. Also, results on tests can be "faked" by a person who knows what to say to get the job. Finally, certain tests may not be legal—so be careful.

4. ...Look for "cookie cutter" people or mirror images of yourself. Yes, new hires need to fit into the corporate culture, but sales requires creativity. Look for imaginative people.

5. ...Consider anyone who is unable to to look you directly in the eye. Nervousness is acceptable, but evasiveness in word or manner is not.

6. ...Rely on intuition alone. This book gives you ways to evaluate people. Use them. You need a systematic approach to interviews. In today's competitive marketplace, you can't afford to make a mistake on hiring.

EVALUATING CANDIDATES

How do you evaluate candidates following the interview? It's clear that the hiring decision is essential to your success. The best way to predict future behavior is by looking at past performance.

In the following pages you will learn how to evaluate a candidate. To start, write down what the job entails, and then consider each candidate's experience in terms of those requirements. Then, answer the other questions. Gradually, a picture of the candidate's suitability for the job will begin to take place. Complete the following for each candidate.

EVALUATING A CANDIDATE

1. This job requires the following characteristics and capabilities:

   a.

   b.

   c.

   d.

Track Record	How This Fits Our Needs

EVALUATING A CANDIDATE (Continued)

2. Write a brief description of the ideal candidate. What skills are needed?

Does this description match any of the people you have interviewed? Can they do the job? Will they do the job? Do they fit the corporate culture?

3. On a scale of 1 to 10 (10 being highest), rate each candidate in the following areas:

   a. Do they have the core elements of strength of personality: charisma, energy, empathy, decisiveness?

      ☐

   b. Do they have high standards of achievement?

      ☐

   c. Are they competitive?

      ☐

   d. Are they thoughtful? Do they see the likely effects of their actions?

      ☐

   e. Do they tailor their approach to suit the personality involved? Are they flexible?

      ☐

   f. Do they have a high tolerance for rejection? How well will they stick with difficult challenges and not quit after meeting refusals?

      ☐

   g. Do they have a knack for explaining complex ideas in simple terms by using examples?

      ☐

Compare the total of the candidates. This may help you reach a hiring decision (or, at the very least, narrow your selection).

HIRING AND THE LAW

Besides your own sound judgment and a good fit between a candidate's goals and those of your organization, you must ensure you stay within the law during the interviewing and hiring process. While you should get professional legal advice for specific circumstances and situations, this section will cover some general rules and describe illegal questions that you must avoid.

Rita Risser, an attorney with McTernan Stender & Walsh of San Jose, California, has provided these guidelines.

1. Watch what you say. Anything you communicate in speech or writing can be considered a legal promise for which you, as an employer, can be held responsible. If the company acts contrary to your word, it can be sued and required to pay money equivalent to past and future lost earnings, including benefits.

2. Watch what you do. Never single out anyone for special treatment. Specifically avoid discrimination on the basis of age, race, color, sex, religion, veteran status and national origin. Also, stay clear of personnel questions relating to any of the following: pregnancy, marital status, physical handicap and medical conditions, including obesity, blood pressure, epilepsy, back problems and AIDS.

3. Watch how you describe compensation. It is especially important to be careful of making a wrong move regarding sales commissions, where there are countless variations of compensation plans. (Note: It is illegal to dock an employee's pay for mistakes or inadvertent errors that cause you to lose money, unless you can prove negligence.)

4. State your company compensation policy and procedures at the time of hire. This is a preventive strategy. It is wise to ask employees to acknowledge—in writing—that they understand the compensation plan before they come on board.

5. Don't ask illegal questions. You can get in serious trouble just by asking seemingly innocent questions that seek information. Questions similar to the following can later be viewed as the basis for a discriminatory decision.

   Examples of such questions are:

   Do you have children?

   Are you married?

   Are you pregnant?

   Can you lift 50 pounds?

   What are your child care arrangements?

   Do you have a college degree?

   Do you have plans to retire?

   What are your salary requirements?

   What was your last salary?

   Are you a citizen?

   Where were you born?

   We work a lot of overtime. Do you have any religious reasons why you can't work Saturdays?

   We have a dress code. Do you have to wear that turban?

   We don't have any other blacks here. Will that make you uncomfortable?

   We have a policy that we only speak English while at work. Do you have a problem with that?

> Remember, it is better not to take chances. If you have any questions regarding what is legal, consult your organization's legal representation first!

MAKING THE HIRING DECISION

Because sales people are such a disparate lot, you need to present your offer in unique ways they will find appealing.

When you make the offer, be absolutely sure you understand what the applicant wants from you as an employer. To help clarify this, list below the four main items you understand the applicant to want, in order of importance:

1.

2.

3.

4.

Match these items up with the 13 most common reasons a person joins a company. If there is no match, you may want to think about whether you may be able to satisfy this person's needs.

REASONS PEOPLE ACCEPT JOB OFFERS

1. Achievement
2. Title
3. Participation
4. Working environment
5. Benefits
6. Salary
7. Bonuses
8. Perks
9. Status
10. Mobility/travel
11. Flexible schedule
12. Independence
13. Recognition

MAKING THE OFFER

Once you've made your choice, bear in mind the following guidelines and cautions.

Guidelines

1. Be flexible. Be prepared to negotiate. You need to know in advance what you are willing to do to hire this candidate, so be prepared to consider special requests. For example, you might need to negotiate flex time for special situations. Make sure you have the authority to negotiate.

2. Make the offer in a relaxed atmosphere. Try to do it somewhere other than under the pressure of a dinner or social function.

3. If your candidate does not accept the job, make sure you find out why. The reason may be important for you to know the next time you make a job offer.

Cautions

1. Never feel rushed to hire someone. The ideal situation is to have people in the pipeline waiting for an opportunity to work for your fine company. Take the time that is necessary and you will never regret it.

2. Don't get into a game of one-upmanship or a bidding war. The kind of character you seek in a person doesn't play games like that. Don't bring yourself down to that level—it's unprofessional.

3. Don't oversell. You know you want the person, but don't cloud your judgment with arrogance. First-class companies court salespeople with the same rigor they use to sell their products. It is easy to come on with too much hype, but remember—you and the employee are in it for the long term, so be straightforward and honest.

CASE STUDY #1
THE TURNOVER DILEMMA

You are sales manager for a medium-sized company. You feel you have done all the right things for your team of salespeople. The pay and benefits are competitive. You have established a quality program, and you have taken a personal interest in your recent hires. Despite this, you are experiencing far more turnover in your sales force than you expect.

Based on what you have read in this book so far, what do you think some of the reasons might be?

What could you do to get additional information?

CHECKING REFERENCES

A flurry of court decisions in recent years has eroded your ability to check references freely. If you need to do this, it is permissible to write for information from past employees. Before you send your letter, have your legal department review it.

Also, consider asking for information from someone other than a former boss. This will give you a fresh, unanticipated look.

Here are some questions you can ask former employers:

1) Describe the work the person did for you.

2) Did you get the result you wanted?

3) Were jobs finished on time? If not, why not?

4) Did the employee understand your business?

5) Was the employee manageable?

6) What were the employee's strengths?

7) Would you rehire the person?

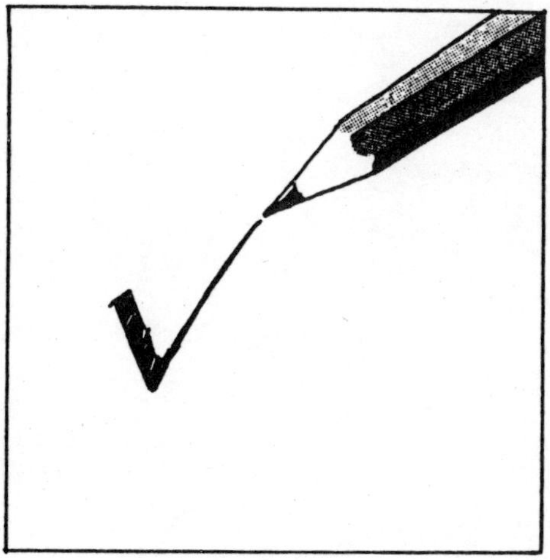

SECTION III

Training

Once you have hired (or inherited) your sales team, it is time to give them a gift, namely, quality training.

You set the stage for success or failure with the approach you take to training. Barbara Pollard was quoted in a recent *College Board News* as saying, "Half of employees who quit, do so within the first 30 days." Keep this statistic in mind and you'll see why it is imperative to instill the right attitude, skills, product knowledge, goals and work habits in new hires. In short, it is important to mold them.

Ferdinand F. Fournies, in his book *Why Employees Don't Do What They're Supposed to Do,* gives the following definition of training as: "Doing what is necessary to deny people who work for you the unpleasant opportunity of failing."

In this section, we will discuss the best ways to train people, how to set objective standards and how to reassure progress.

GETTING OFF TO A GOOD START

An Wang, the founder of Wang Computers, once said, "I find it surprising that so many talented people derail themselves one way or another during their lives." Good training will get a person started on the right track. Training really does set the stage for the years ahead in the life of every employee. If you conduct training thoughtfully, you may prevent a derailment.

Training salespeople starts with getting them comfortable with relating to other people (potential customers) and continues by getting them comfortable with what they're selling (product).

Complete the following outline to determine how you plan to get new hires off to a good start. Write down the five most important items you plan to cover in each of these areas.

1. Getting comfortable with other people

   a.

   b.

   c.

   d.

   e.

> Remember that sales is primarily a *people* activity. How your sales force comes across personally to your customers makes all the difference.

2. Getting comfortable with product knowledge

   a.

   b.

   c.

   d.

   e.

> Some topics are basic for your salespeople to know. What information will enable them to put customers at ease and help to build their product knowledge base more rapidly?

PUTTING YOUR TRAINING PLAN TOGETHER

So far, you've been asked to address only the most basic aspects of training (people and products). The heart of superior training involves much more detailed information and skills.

Following is a list of general areas to cover in your training program. Fill in each blank to specify what your salespeople basically need to know. Then check the box at right when you have prepared this information for inclusion into the program.

Area	What salespeople need to know	Ready to incorporate into training program?
1. Key benefits of product or service	______________________	☐
2. Prospecting guidelines	______________________	☐
3. Making initial contacts	______________________	☐
4. Qualification of prospects	______________________	☐
5. Handling objections	______________________	☐
6. Closing the sale	______________________	☐
7. (Others) __________	______________________	☐
8. ______________	______________________	☐

KEYS TO TRAINING SALESPEOPLE

Want to have top-flight customer sales? There is a well-known "secret" for making this happen: hire and train top-flight salespeople! We all know that customers "improve" in direct proportion to the quality of the salesperson covering that account.

Here are four keys to help you train great salespeople:

1. **Involve them from the start.** Rather than talk *at* your people, allow them to participate. Psychological studies show that even very smart people will fail to learn without proper instruction. An important component of proper instruction is meaningful interaction between students and teacher.

2. **Make sure everyone has a mentor.** The best mentor is someone who is a master at the activity being taught. For some of your people that may be you. For others it may be a veteran performer. New people need to learn from someone who is seasoned, because without experience, the uniqueness of your product or service cannot be communicated. Let them observe you or the mentor that has been selected in action.

3. **Consider training to be continuous.** The key to repeated success and sustained growth is a constant upgrading of skills and knowledge. Winners always work harder on themselves than they do on the job.

4. **Watch yourself—everyone else does!** As a manager, you can never underestimate your personal impact. Take pains never to lose your self-confidence, enthusiasm, willingness to help. Everything you do or say will be noticed.

A TWO DAY TRAINING PROGRAM

When you hire new salespeople, there are some basic points that need to be covered. Following is a suggested two-day training program that incorporates basic information that new hires should have. Modify it to meet your specific needs.

FIRST DAY

The main topics of the first day are:

a) company history and strengths

b) why profitable relationships with customers are essential

c) and why professionalism is the standard.

The first day should provide a vision of the future company. It is important for new salespeople to know how the sales operation will contribute to the vision. Such things as dress, ethics, and other expectations for sales people should be covered.

Since each organization is different, it is important to set your own objectives in covering the issues. Write three in the space provided that you feel should be accomplished in your first day:

a.

b.

c.

It is also important to insure your new hires become familiar with basic product knowledge, skills, attitudes, goals and work habits as quickly as possible. Case studies that exemplify these items can be effective. Create several cases in advance of the training session and cover them during the first day. Properly done, these cases will provide a good overview of your expectations.

Professional buyers tell us time and again that nothing turns them off quicker than sales representatives who don't communicate what makes their product or service unique and valuable.

Following is a way you can help instill your product/service uniqueness. After a thorough discussion of your organization's attributes, ask each trainee to write five things that make your company unique in the marketplace.

1.

2.

3.

4.

5.

*For an excellent book on this topic, order *New Employee Orientation* using the information in the back of this book.

TRAINING (Continued)

SECOND DAY

On the second day, you should provide an overview in the following six areas:

1) a market overview
2) product knowledge
3) basic sales skills requirements
4) attitude
5) goals/quotas and expectations
6) work habits/requirements (reports, etc.)

1. **Sales situations:** Try the case-study method. Use realistic cases made up in advance—either your own, or those developed by experienced salespeople. Cover subjects similar to the following:

- discovering and developing a new account
- handling a difficult customer
- discussing a situation involving a tough ethical decision
- learning how to service accounts
- dealing effectively with competition
- reacting to changes in the marketplace

To effectively use case studies

1. Have salespeople read the case.
2. Meet informally as a small group with a discussion facilitator.
3. Present group conclusion to the entire group.

There are several benefits to using a case approach:

1. It allows for discussion about such things as company philosophy and values.
2. Case studies demonstrate the real world of selling.
3. It is a great way for people to get to know each other.
4. Properly conducted, this approach can build confidence in new people, and boost morale.
5. As people share ideas during the exercise, it gives you as manager an advance look at how your new people reason and react to realistic situations.

2. Product knowledge: Salespeople need solid, basic product knowledge. It is essential for their confidence, and the confidence customers place in them. Have trainees list the four most important aspects of your product or service, and ask them to write out why they are important.

Once your people understand the foundation of your business, they will put customers at ease and begin to build their product knowledge even more rapidly.

3. People skills: Professional buyers agree that they become annoyed by sales representatives who don't demonstrate good selling skills. This section of your sales training should cover the following topics, *as they apply to your business:*

a) prospecting
b) initial contact
c) qualifications
d) objections
e) closing

Consider ordering *Professional Selling* by Rebecca Morgan. It is a book similar to the one you are reading that covers professional selling skills. A form in the back of this book lists it, plus several other helpful titles.

Remind your trainees that, above all, sales is a *people* business. To help them clarify their goals in the sales skills section, ask them to list four "people skills" they plan to use when selling. After all, how your sales force comes across to customers will make all the difference.

TRAINING (Continued)

4. **Attitude:** A positive and productive attitude is crucial to sales success. Your people need to know why it is important to be in the right frame of mind when they prospect and sell.

This part of training should extend into the day-to-day world of work. New hires should go on sales calls with yourself or other professionals where a positive attitude is demonstrated and stressed.

5. **Goals:** During this portion of training you need to emphasize the importance of both company and personal goals. They need to hear that you and they will discuss and set goals on an ongoing basis. To stimulate and improve the performance of your salespeople, you must insure the goals and standards you set are understood and agreed to by them.

Salespeople need to know what is expected of them. Measure them only against themselves—*not* against star performers or other divisions. Winning means setting a plan for each person, and then helping them achieve or beat that plan.

EXERCISE: TRAINING SALESPEOPLE

This is a good exercise to give to new salespeople once they have completed their basic training. It allows you to test them after you have provided the information you will ask them to complete. If they can't complete this exercise to your satisfaction, don't go any farther with them until you have reevaluated your training program. Ask each trainee to list:

BENEFITS TO THE CONSUMER

Three Reasons to Buy From Me:

1. ______________________________
____
2. ______________________________
____
3. ______________________________
____

Three Reasons to Buy From My Company:

1. ______________________________
____
2. ______________________________
____
3. ______________________________
____

Three Reasons My Product/Service Will Meet Your Needs:

1. ______________________________
____
2. ______________________________
____
3. ______________________________
____

RATE YOURSELF AS A SALES TRAINER

Even if your company uses outside sales training or has a training department, you as sales manager are the most important source of training for your sales team. Only if you have the skills and qualities that allow you to oversee profitable relationships with customers can you convey a sense of professionalism while training.

Go over the following checklist and determine how you feel about each quality or skill. Then work to improve areas where you need improvement. You might ask your manager to rate the items on this list so you can compare your assessment against his or hers.

QUALITY OR SKILL	YES	IMPROVE	NO
1. Demonstrates patience, tolerance	☐	☐	☐
2. Knows product well	☐	☐	☐
3. Communicates to be understood: clearly and concisely	☐	☐	☐
4. Is motivated to train	☐	☐	☐
5. Shows empathy, care and concern	☐	☐	☐
6. Is confident of abilities	☐	☐	☐
7. Gives clear instructions, making the complex simple	☐	☐	☐
8. Creates a good learning environment	☐	☐	☐
9. Is organized and prepared	☐	☐	☐
10. Has a relaxed aura of total self-acceptance	☐	☐	☐

TRAINING NEVER ENDS

The key to meeting your goals and allowing your people constantly to improve is continuous training. You fare best when you hire people who work even harder on improving themselves than they do on the job. Your role then is to give them every opportunity to learn and grow.

School is never out for the professional. Author of one of the earliest sales books, Frank Bettger (*How I Raised Myself from Failure to Success in Sales*) was asked why he continued to study and work so hard when he was 78 years old.

''Because,'' he replied, ''there is so much I need to learn.''

This is the attitude you should look for in your sales people. The easiest way to keep training your people is by working with them closely, on a daily basis, making on-the-spot corrections and comments.

SECTION IV

Motivating and Managing Salespeople

The following pages will give you the building blocks to lay the foundation of a solid management structure. You will learn how to establish a climate of mutual respect. And you will see that by paying continuous attention to your people, you will gather the necessary information to make quality decisions.

POSITIVE MOTIVATION

As a sales manager, you can motivate your sales force in many ways. Countless studies and personal experiences of successful sales managers prove time and again that praising people for desirable behavior is much more effective in increasing and maintaining productivity than criticism and fault finding. Take the following test to see how you rate as a positive manager.

	YES	NO
1. Do you prefer to "catch people doing something right" instead of waiting them out to make a mistake?	☐	☐
2. Do you set a positive example for your sales force?	☐	☐
3. Do you communicate in a straightforward manner so your team does not have to guess about what you expect?	☐	☐
4. Do you always give credit to your people when they deserve it?	☐	☐
5. When someone does something wrong, do you constructively say, "In the future, we should..." instead of merely criticizing them?	☐	☐
6. Do you give your people an opportunity to grow in their jobs by providing new opportunities and challenges?	☐	☐
7. Do you ask your employees to evaluate you? Do you encourage their feedback?	☐	☐

For every "no" answer, think about how you could turn it to a "yes" for yourself. Being a positive motivator will increase your productivity tremendously!

SET A GOOD EXAMPLE

A well known slogan is, "I can't hear what you're saying because your actions are so loud." This means that the way you go about your business sets an example every day in every way. It really doesn't matter what you *say*—it's what you *do* that counts.

Effective management requires a combination of personal qualities that guide your behavior. Your objective should be to set an example of sales excellence. The following list of qualities will help you to rate yourself on setting a good example for your sales team. Check those you feel you do on a regular basis.

I strive to:

- ☐ Court my employees, never forgetting their needs.
- ☐ Show how much I care for them as individuals.
- ☐ Remain committed to solutions and never allow poor performance to go unnoticed.
- ☐ Stress teamwork and cooperation.
- ☐ Promote competition against realistic measurable standards of excellence.
- ☐ Exemplify a service attitude by supporting your team both inside the organization and with customers.
- ☐ Honor individual differences among team members and teach them to capitalize on their strengths and improve their weak points.

SET A GOOD EXAMPLE (Continued)

- ☐ Treat ordinary people like they are extraordinary.
- ☐ Teach team members by example to work both hard *and* smart.
- ☐ Make effective use of resources, such as time and expense money.
- ☐ Persist in the face of obstacles, finding ways to work around handicaps.
- ☐ Constantly update product knowledge and market conditions.
- ☐ Stay focused on the objectives I have set—both individually and for the team.
- ☐ Remain open to feedback, especially constructive criticism.
- ☐ Keep everyone (including myself) ambitious.

CONCENTRATE ON PRODUCTIVITY

Peter Drucker, the spokesperson of modern management, said, "The company that systematically concentrates on its productivity is bound to gain competitive advantage."

Productivity comes from focusing on success. One way to accomplish this is to celebrate every time a goal is met. Create some excitement, have fun! Reinforce strengths, and work on improving weaknesses. When people are performing poorly the following five things might help you return the focus to productivity.

You should:

1. Ask their understanding of what is supposed to happen. Let others state their position first. Learn what their perception of the situation is. They will more readily accept your suggestions for improvement if they feel you are willing to hear their assessment first.

2. Get agreement on a course of action to improve the situation. Make sure you get in writing *who* is responsible for doing *what* by *when*. Above all, keep your focus on the action to be taken and not on blaming others for creating the problem.

3. Use tact. Keep personalities out of the discussion and focus instead on business solutions. Remember it's how you say it *as well* as what is said.

4. Remember that a problem is usually caused by one of the following (each is matched with its own solution): ignorance (provide information), awareness (focus attention), practice (change the system or behavior) or market conditions (adapt your strategy).

5. Always choose the right time and place to point out a weakness. There is never an excuse to humiliate anyone, especially in front of other employees.

Your job is to create an atmosphere of mutual respect. In particular, the employee's self-respect must remain intact at all times.

PROSPECTING

Prospecting is one of the important parts of a new salesperson's training. There are two types of prospecting.

1) referral
2) non-referral

Referral is absolutely the best system. When training new hires, teach each salesperson to specifically ask for names of future potential clients following each transaction with a new, or existing, customer.

Non-referral prospecting is more difficult, but can be very successful. It is a systematic approach broken into six steps of qualification of the prospect. These steps include:

1. Determine sources which make prospecting sense

2. Find ways to make an initial contact (mail, phone, etc.)

3. Establish contact

4. Qualify the prospect to make sure he/she is worth a follow-up

5. Determine how to initiate the selling process.

CLOSING

When you were starting in sales, you may have learned that closing was a *technique*. This is no longer the case. All the old ''rules'' surrounding closing have changed. Closing is no longer a technique that you ''use'' on a customer, it is now a key part of the sales process. The difference is not one of semantics. It is so important that understanding closing may make the difference between having repeat business or having none.

Closing is an *attitude*—not a set of skills. The important thing to remember is that your goal is to move the customers through the sales process in order to reach a decision, after they have the necessary information.

Author Rebecca Morgan has an excellent discussion of closing attitudes in her book *Professional Selling*. This title may be ordered using the form in the back of this book. For now, though, the important point to instill in the awareness of your trainees is that at every point in the sales process, they must ask for *some* action. An action that will lead to some further action and eventually close the sale. Remind your salespeople that they are not ''professional visitors''—they have a mission to accomplish.

Don't sell asking for some action on the part of the customer short. Westinghouse increased their sales by 25 percent in one year by making it mandatory for the sales force to request *some* action on the customer's part at the end of each discussion.

Whatever you do, respect the intelligence of your prospects. Customers are too sophisticated today to be manipulated by ''closing techniques.'' If you do a good job of listening to their needs and then presenting solutions throughout the sales process, they will make the best decision, in accordance with your abilities and the facts presented. To underscore this important point: Closing is not a technique, it's an *attitude*.

HOW TO SUSTAIN HIGH PERFORMANCE

Did you ever notice in a football game that when a team gets within 10 yards of the goal, it is suddenly much harder for it to score? Such may also be the case with salespeople. Even when star performers get on a roll, it's not easy for them to stay there.

How do you sustain high output from your best producers? Mary Kay Ash of Mary Kay Cosmetics has one of the best answers: she would "praise her people to the skies" every chance she got.

Top performers never work for money alone. They crave recognition and ego satisfaction as well. Good management of these people is largely common sense: listen well, tell them what you expect, give them the necessary tools and training and then get out of the way.

Here are three things to remember to help your salespeople sustain high performance:

1. Never separate accountability from responsibility. If you give your top performers autonomy, make sure they continue to hit all of their performance goals. Measure them! Every top performer needs a coach and a cheerleader to help sustain performance. Give your players what they need.

2. Recognize them constantly. Keep them informed. Never ignore them. Spend time with them at every opportunity. Talk about their performance, and keep their "busy work" to a minimum. Celebrate every time a goal is met.

3. Create an environment for success. Provide your top performers with additional training to keep them motivated and challenged. The biggest room in life is the room for improvement. Keep the environment full of opportunities and high energy. Good people can't be overtrained.

SALES MANAGER'S TROUBLESHOOTING GUIDE

PERFORMANCE PROBLEM	POSSIBLE SOLUTION
Sales are slumping.	Ask employees their ideas to solve the problem. Pinpoint reasons for sales slippage and attack problems with a fresh strategy. Be pro-active.
People are reluctant to talk about problems.	Maintain contact. This allows you to build up a rapport and observe first hand what is going on. People will feel comfortable coming to you if they know your job is to understand and support them.
Lack of motivation.	Pride and recognition are the best motivators. They can help create peer pressure that will steer individuals toward higher productivity.
Needed changes are not taking place.	Find out why. If someone says, "We always have done things this way," have a heart-to-heart talk with that person to explain the reasons for change and get agreement to "buy in"—or at least give change a try.

SALES MANAGER'S TROUBLESHOOTING GUIDE (Continued)

PERFORMANCE PROBLEM	POSSIBLE SOLUTION
Mistakes keep occurring.	Review what is causing mistakes to recur. Obtain agreement about a revised course of action and retrain if necessary.
You are making poor decisions.	Stop making quick decisions. Slow down and allow intuition and emotion to add a dimension to your decisions that those made by logic alone often lack. Listen to other points of view.
You are losing credibility as a manager.	Review your practices. Ask your team for feedback. Invite dissent. Review your objectives to see if they are still realistic. Modify them if necessary.
Morale is low.	Let your team know where they fit in the big picture. Give them a mission. Challenge another group to a baseball game (or darts, or trivia contest). Reinforce the sense of belonging to a winning organization.

SALES MANAGER'S TROUBLESHOOTING GUIDE (Continued)

PERFORMANCE PROBLEM	POSSIBLE SOLUTION
Sales strategies are not working.	Although it is a mistake to change sales goals constantly, don't be afraid to try some new things. Encourage creativity. Have a long-term marketing program that can be adapted to changing times. Be realistic—but be flexible.
Your top sales producer slacks off.	Appeal to his or her sense of pride. Praise past victories. Pinpoint causes. Provide additional support. Extend some new challenges.

SELF ASSESSMENT

Here are 20 descriptions that will help you measure principles of management and motivation. Rate yourself to see where you would need to work on upgrading your rating.

As a sales manager, I feel I have:

	EXCELLENT	AVERAGE	NEED IMPROVEMENT
1. Courage of conviction.	☐	☐	☐
2. The ability to see things from others' perspectives.	☐	☐	☐
3. Skill in creating and managing change.	☐	☐	☐
4. Persistence and endurance.	☐	☐	☐
5. Realistic goals and expectations.	☐	☐	☐
6. A sense of humor.	☐	☐	☐
7. Trust in myself and others.	☐	☐	☐
8. Solid decision-making abilities.	☐	☐	☐
9. The wisdom to use power wisely.	☐	☐	☐
10. Commitment (without this, all else is meaningless).	☐	☐	☐
11. The ability to get ideas across.	☐	☐	☐
12. Respect—both self and from others.	☐	☐	☐
13. A goal-oriented purpose.	☐	☐	☐
14. Cooperation from all levels within my organization.	☐	☐	☐
15. Discipline. I can control my behavior that ensures things get done.	☐	☐	☐
16. The ability to recognize the value of others.	☐	☐	☐
17. The desire to praise others for a job well done. (Even criticism can build confidence when accompanied by praise.)	☐	☐	☐
18. Superior listening skills.	☐	☐	☐
19. The ability to take reasonable risks.	☐	☐	☐
20. A problem-solving approach to situations.	☐	☐	☐

FOSTERING A HIGH PRODUCTIVITY ENVIRONMENT

For a successful sales manager, the bottom line is keeping productivity high. Do you value the factors that create a high productivity environment? See how many of the conditions listed below are part of your sales force's everyday experience. Check the response that you think most closely fits your operation's environment. Be honest!

	YES	NO
1. The work is challenging.	☐	☐
2. Everyone's opinion counts.	☐	☐
3. Compensation is clearly tied to performance.	☐	☐
4. Performance is measured fairly.	☐	☐
5. People have autonomy.	☐	☐
6. The environment is competitive.	☐	☐
7. Clear goals have been established.	☐	☐
8. People have an opportunity to learn.	☐	☐
9. There is a feeling of teamwork.	☐	☐
10. People can earn special incentives.	☐	☐

If you could check "yes" to at least seven of the 10 items, you are on your way to creating a climate that encourages productivity and allows your people to do their best work. Congratulations!

QUOTAS AND INCENTIVES—1

Salespeople are, by definition, competitive. They like to be challenged and need targets that they can aim for. One way you can help keep them motivated and productive is through the use of well designed quotas. Giving people a goal can be very effective, but, take care. Quotas must be designed so they will also help the company achieve its objectives.

Getting your sales force running hard in the wrong direction can put a real strain on your company. Make sure quotas emphasize the right *kind* of sales, the markets you want to *target*, the *products* you want to feature and the *strategic profit goals* of the company.

Following are three key concepts to keep in mind when setting quotas that were developed by nationally known sales trainer Jim Pancero of Cincinnati:

1. **Examine the potential of the assigned area.** You can't get hot water out of the cold-water tap. You want to set your goals to stretch performance, but not beyond what is humanly possible. Always keep the characteristics of the sales territory in mind.

2. **Evaluate what was done before.** Increases are always possible, but what size should you expect? Use historical records in the territory as a gauge in setting quotas. Small successes by meeting realizable quotas will build confidence in a salesperson, and ultimately, bigger successes. Set quotas accordingly.

3. **Examine the talent of the person to whom you're giving the quota.** The biggest mistake you can make is failing to recognize the individuality of each salesperson. The key to productivity is uncovering strengths, and capitalizing on them. Ask your salespeople to do more of what they're already good at, and you'll get the highest productivity.

Pancero says, "Think of your quota like a rubber band. You need the right rubber band for the job. You want it to stretch, but you don't want it to break."

QUOTAS AND INCENTIVES—2

Effective quotas and incentives can inspire salespeople to produce beyond the bare minimum, but don't ask for the impossible. When you set up your quota for each salesperson, the following checklist might help.

	YES	COULD BE IMPROVED	NO
1. Does meeting this quota contribute to meeting the sales and profit goals of the company?	☐	☐	☐
2. Have I built in flexibility so this quota can be modified if necessary?	☐	☐	☐
3. Has the salesperson contributed to the setting of his or her goals?	☐	☐	☐
4. Is the goal based on the salesperson's past performance?	☐	☐	☐
5. Will meeting this quota represent a stretch for this salesperson?	☐	☐	☐
6. Does this quota truly allow the measurement of the salesperson's performance?	☐	☐	☐
7. Is the quota specific enough to spread so ongoing measurement makes sense. Is it flexible enough to take into account legitimate unexpected circumstances?	☐	☐	☐
8. Will the salesperson consider the quota challenging and attainable?	☐	☐	☐
9. If the salesperson helped set the standard, has it been reviewed to insure it is realistic?	☐	☐	☐
10. Have I accounted for market changes when setting the quota, so it can be adjusted upward if extraordinary events push sales through the roof?	☐	☐	☐

SECTION V

Evaluating Your Sales Team

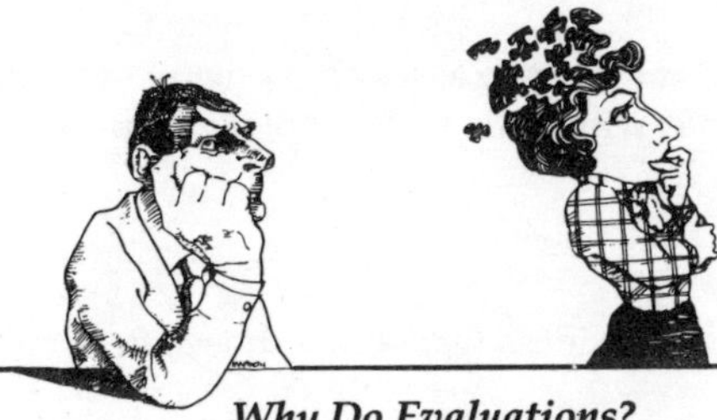

Why Do Evaluations?

If you knew of something you could do to improve the performance of your people, would you hesitate a moment before doing it? Probably not. Yet many sales managers miss an important opportunity to use personal evaluations to do just that.

Productivity can be designed into our sales system almost instantly—through evaluations. Evaluations provide a way to track the progress of all of your staff.

Psychological Associates Inc. of St. Louis surveyed 4,000 salespeople at 190 companies and found that 70% reported they didn't have a clear picture of what was expected from them or where they stood within their companies.

In this section you will learn how to do a quality evaluation. You will learn how to conduct a job appraisal, reward performance, compensate employees, promote them, terminate them. Read on!

COMMUNICATION

Lee Iacocca said that when he was asked how Chrysler was able to make more money in six years under his leadership than during the previous 60 years, he replied: ''Communication is everything.''

So it is for you. You need to be in regular contact with your people. You can accomplish this through regular phone calls, through required written reports, and by going on sales calls with them.

In face-to-face communications, it is best to let them know you as a ''real'' person. Listen well, and ask their opinions often. Pay attention to what they tell you. Learn their personal philosophies and their strengths. The better you understand them is probably *the* most important factor in getting things done by them over time.

When you have critical information to deliver, ensure it is in writing, even if you deliver it personally. Request a sales report be turned in weekly that records sales calls and the progress on each.

Check the following important areas to assess how many of them you regularly and clearly comunicate about with your salespeople. I request and/or provide information concerning:

☐ Changes occurring in the business (especially those affecting sales)

☐ Developments and trends in the market

☐ Corporate goals and how well they are being met

☐ Decisions that are pending (Get them involved whenever possible)

☐ Customer feedback on your product and that of the competition

WEEKLY REPORT OF OUTSIDE CALLS

SALESPERSON	DISTRICT OFFICE	WEEK ENDING Mo. / Day / Yr.	REGIONAL MANAGER	REPORT NO.

DATE	NAME AND CITY OF PROSPECT OR CUSTOMER	CUSTOMER	PROSPECT	(✓) if first visit prospect	INDIVIDUAL CONTACTED	COMMENTS
	TOTAL CALLS THIS WEEK ►					
	TOTAL CALLS THIS MONTH ►					
	TOTAL CALLS THIS YTD ►					

HOW TO CONDUCT A PERFORMANCE APPRAISAL

The purpose of a performance review is not only to help the employee understand what is expected and how he or she is doing relative to those expectations, but also to increase productivity and company loyalty. Performance reviews done properly also reduce the chances that an employee terminated for performance problems could successfully sue the company.

Seven steps can help you discuss performance with an employee:

Step 1: Listen to your employee's self-appraisal before offering an evaluation. Then, give a balanced picture of an employee's strengths and weaknesses from a written document that has been carefully prepared.

Step 2: Analyze what you are going to say. You want to be tactful and sensitive—remember, your job is to motivate, not destroy.

Step 3: Discuss differences and offer specific suggestions on how to capitalize on strong points and improve weaknesses. Work with the salesperson to develop realistic goals.

Step 4: If a disagreement occurs, listen closely and ask for specific facts. Don't become defensive. State your position directly and clearly. If necessary, take a cooling-off period—possibly a couple of days. Keep in mind the Chinese proverb that 1,000 years of good will can be undone by one word. So don't allow an emotional situation to get out of control.

Step 5: Reviews should never contain surprises. If you constantly reinforce and give feedback on a regular basis, no one will be surprised. The appraisal is a chance to fine tune. For instance, go over one thing a top performer may benefit from working on. Approach it positively. For example, if they don't contribute enough at sales meetings, say, "I'm concerned the group is not getting the benefit of your experience and want you to consider the following presentation at our next meeting."

Step 6: Don't become a therapist! If any personal problems surface during the discussion that need more professional help, listen with empathy, then help them find appropriate help.

Step 7: Don't tie salaries or bonuses directly to the review period. Money not only depends on the person's performance, but also on the financial conditions of the company, the economy and what the competition is doing. If you incorporate money with a review, the employee may have expectations that you are unable to meet. Ensure your employee understands that compensation decisions include review results—along with many other factors—and that the review alone is not the basis for salary or bonus action.

The next two pages (62-63) contain an excellent *Performance Appraisal Checklist for Managers* reprinted by permission from *Effective Performance Appraisal* by Robert Maddux. This fine book can be ordered using the form in the back of this book.

A PERFORMANCE APPRAISAL CHECK LIST FOR MANAGERS

The following check list is designed to guide the manager in preparing, conducting and following through on employee performance appraisal discussions.

I PERSONAL PREPARATION

☐ I have reviewed mutually understood expectations for job duties, projects, goals, standards and any other predetermined performance factors pertinent to this appraisal discussion.

☐ I have observed job performance measured against mutually understood expectations. In so doing, I have done my best to avoid such pitfalls as:
- ______ Bias/prejudice
- ______ Memory lapses
- ______ Overattention to some aspects of the job at the expense of others
- ______ Being overly influenced by my own experience
- ______ Trait evaluation rather than performance measurement

☐ I have reviewed the employee's background including:
- ______ Skills
- ______ Work experience
- ______ Training

☐ I have determined the employee's performance strengths and areas in need of improvement and in doing so have:
- ______ Accumulated specific, unbiased documentation that can be used to help communicate my position
- ______ Limited myself to critical points
- ______ Prepared a possible development plan in case the employee needs assistance

☐ I have identified areas for concentration in setting goals and standards for the next appraisal period.

☐ I have given the employee advance notice of when the discussion will be held so that he/she can prepare.

☐ I have set aside an adequate block of uninterrupted time to permit a full and complete discussion.

II CONDUCTING THE APPRAISAL DISCUSSION

☐ I plan to begin the discussion by creating a sincere, open and friendly atmosphere. This includes:

_____ Reviewing the purpose of the discussion
_____ Making it clear that is a joint discussion for the purpose of mutual problem-solving and goal setting
_____ Striving to put the employee at ease

☐ In the body of the discussion I intend to keep the focus on job performance and related factors. This includes:

_____ Discussing job requirements—employee strengths, accomplishments, improvement needs and evaluating results of performance against objectives set during previous reviews and discussions
_____ Being prepared to cite observations for each point I want to discuss
_____ Encouraging the employee to appraise his/her own performance
_____ Using open, reflective and directive questions to promote thought, understanding and problem solving

☐ I will encourage the employee to outline his/her personal plans for self-development before suggesting ideas of my own. In the process, I will:

_____ Encourage the employee to set personal growth and improvement targets
_____ Strive to reach agreement on appropriate development plans that detail what the employee intends to do, a timetable and support I am prepared to give

☐ I am prepared to discuss work assignments, projects and goals for the next appraisal period and will ask the employee to come prepared with suggestions.

III CLOSING THE DISCUSSION

☐ I will be prepared to make notes, summarize agreements and follow up. In closing, I will:

_____ Summarize what has been discussed
_____ Show enthusiasm for plans that have been made
_____ Give the employee an opportunity to make additional suggestions
_____ End on a positive, friendly, harmonious note

IV POST-APPRAISAL FOLLOW UP

☐ As soon as the discussion is over, I will record the plans made, points requiring follow up, the commitments I made, and provide a copy for the employee.

☐ I will also evaluate how I handled the discussion.

_____ What I did well
_____ What I could have done better
_____ What I learned about the employee and his/her job
_____ What I learned about myself and my job

FOLLOWING UP—THREE SUGGESTIONS

1 WRITTEN RECORDS

Once the performance appraisal discussion has been concluded, a manager should immediately make a written record of:

— The overall appraisal for the previous period;

— Plans that both parties agreed to;

— Any personal commitments requiring specific action.

A copy of this summary should be given to the employee.

2 REFLECTION

Following each review is a good time to review your performance in leading the discussion. Some good questions are:

— What was done well?

— What was done poorly?

— What will be done differently next time?

— What was learned about the employee?

— What was learned about self and job?

3 FOLLOW THROUGH

A third element of follow up is to insure that agreements are kept and plans followed. If this is not done, the entire appraisal loses its impact and the employee assumes no one cares very much about performance. This phase of the follow up is the initial phase of the next appraisal.

TWO KEYS TO SUPERIOR PERFORMANCE

Lots of things add up to superior performance, but two key characteristics are most common to individuals who excel as salespeople.

The first is consistency.

In a superior salesperson, consistency means:

a) Maintaining a positive attitude—even when things aren't going well

b) Making prospecting a regular daily activity

c) Establishing high personal performance standards and maintaining them

d) Dispensing information correctly and factually

e) Being considered by customers as an ally who can help solve their problems

f) Tying the close of a sale to needs and benefits

The second is persistence.

Persistence in selling means:

a) Doing the entire job of selling (including paperwork)

b) Systematic follow up with all prospects

c) Emotional satisfaction from making a sale

d) Effective use of resources, including time

e) Working around handicaps until the problem is solved

f) Continual updating of knowledge and marketplace

Emphasize consistency and persistence in evaluations. Keeping your sales force focused on these two qualities will make a positive difference in their performance.

RECOGNIZING AND ADDRESSING PROBLEMS

It is usually a tough task to confront a problem behavior in a person, but it is necessary. As much as you might like, problems don't and won't go away if ignored. As a sales manager, you have to be able to say to your people, "We have certain job requirements for all members of the sales team—and by accepting your job, you are agreeing to fulfill these obligations. We cannot compromise on issues such as attendance, honesty or your ability to deliver minimum results."

Following are some common problems and their possible solutions:

PROBLEM	POSSIBLE SOLUTION
Inability to get along with co-workers or customers	Arrange a meeting with customers or co-workers to find out what specific behaviors are creating the problem. Then counsel your salesperson to make the required behavioral change. If your salesperson does not or cannot respond to the problem, he or she may be in the wrong line of work and need to be reassigned or terminated. Selling, after all, is a "people business."
Incompetence	Get the facts. Some incompetence may be due to inexperience and can be corrected through training. Normally it is possible for a person (through supervised practice) to learn the required skills.
Dishonesty	Dishonest employees cannot be tolerated. Legally, any act of dishonesty is cause for immediate dismissal. It is good policy to have employees sign an acknowledgment to this effect when they are hired. If you fire a dishonest employee *make sure* you have the documented facts. Otherwise you could end up with legal problems! Never terminate anyone unless it has been thoroughly discussed with your superiors.

PROBLEM	POSSIBLE SOLUTION
Poor attitude	This can be tricky. Often those with a poor attitude are not aware of their problem and the effect it has on others. You need to respond to the needs and feelings of your employees. Discover what their perceptions are, listen and offer constructive suggestions for improvement. Monitor the situation to ensure the problem employee does not drift back into negative territory.
Lack of motivation	If you know you are providing the right environment for productivity, then the problem belongs to the employee. Like attitude, motivation comes mainly from within. A frank discussion that lets your employee know you are aware of his or her situation and an offer to help them resolve the problem is usually the best solution. They must understand it is ultimately their responsibility to keep themselves motivated.

The five problems presented are the major reasons sales people get fired, according to the Robert Half recruiting company. Can you think of three additional problems you are facing or have faced recently? Based on what you've learned, what do you believe your best solutions to be?

Problem 1.

Solution

Problem 2.

Solution

Problem 3.

Solution

COMPENSATION GUIDELINES

You must design your compensation program around your specific industry, the competition and the skills and experience of your salespeople.

Often, a good ratio of commission to salary is 65 to 35, according to a study by A.M.P. Inc. in an article in the *Across the Board* magazine. This, however, will differ considerably depending on your company or industry. Following are some guidelines to use when designing your compensation package. All such programs should be carefully reviewed with the appropriate managers within your organization before any announcements are made.

Cash

Cash awards are delicate. If you design a program in which cash incentives favor the top producers on the assumption that they will produce more, you may be fooling yourself. Top producers normally will be top producers under just about any circumstance. Try to concentrate on areas that will bring you the best returns. All awards should be tied directly to performance results.

Non cash

If you can design a compensation program that combines both pay for performance and non monetary rewards that create employee satisfaction, then you will encourage loyal and committed salespeople. Salespeople are motivated by recognition—plaques, dinners, awards and trips. Be prepared to change award programs, according to new goals and objectives.

Incentives

If you set up a trip to a resort location include the salesperson's spouse or friend. This arrangement keeps the person's home and personal support system involved and motivates the employee.

You can also do such things as:

- display pictures of top producers in a prominent place for top achievers.
- form a club for top achievers.
- recognize top producers at special recognition affairs or other events such as corporate board meetings.
- give out recognition gifts that show respect to the individual for their accomplishments. Even something as simple as flowers to a spouse or significant other can make a difference.

Rewarding Veterans—a Special Case

Successful salespeople who have long experience are a tough group to reward. The carrot-and-stick approach is not as effective with them as it once was. So for veterans, consider awards such as ''lifetime quotas'' or ''X million dollar roundtable.'' Challenge them to new heights. Show them what an asset they are by having a special ''honor club'' for veterans. This sets the tone of commitment and respect for persistence in the corporate culture, because ''rookies'' will observe how you treat your senior people.

> ''Keep the right goal in mind. Salespeople don't look for money, but for applause. If you create something of value to them, the sales will come.''
>
> —Robert Ronstadt
> C.E.O., Lord Publishing

CORRECTING/ADJUSTING COMPENSATION

Here's an opportunity to review some common compensation problems. See if you're making any of them. It is always better to correct situations sooner than later. If you wait, sometimes it can be too late.

Mistakes:

1. Copying someone else's compensation program (especially from a different industry). Every sales force is different, so address the business and industry you are in. Company size, profitability, environmental outlook and other factors must also be considered.

2. Setting unrealistic goals. Make sure what you ask your people to do represents a challenge—but ensure it isn't outside the realm of possibility either. If experience shows a goal is unrealistic (either too high or too low), adjust it with the help of your experienced team members.

3. Sales goals that aren't tied into company profits. Sales goals, to be effective in the long run, must be part of the big picture. That means if sales goals are met, they will contribute to the profit goals of the company.

4. Plans are rigid and unresponsive to changing conditions. Commitment does not mean inflexibility. While you must persevere in your commitment to having your sales force meet its goals, you must allow for changes in circumstances and respond accordingly.

5. Using the same criteria for yourself as for your salespeople. Your job is different than those of the people you manage. Their job is to get sales; your job is to manage and motivate them. It's usually a mistake to be "one of the group" as far as compensation plans go.

Now, take an honest look at two mistakes you might be making regarding compensation, and develop solutions for these problems.

Problem	**Solution**
1.	
2.	

TERMINATIONS

Terminations are never easy. Early preparation for this unpleasant but nevertheless real possibility is essential in today's world. To make your life easier, make your hires provisional for a period of time (usually 3-6 months). Set some realistic goals and follow them up with a 30-day activity report. This will help alert you to any ''red flags'' early.

When you recognize a red flag—react. No one can improve until he or she knows a problem exists. Additionally, if you need to fire them at a later date and cannot document that your employee was advised about the reason for the termination and given an opportunity to correct the problem, your chances of having the termination stick are minimal. Document everything!

If you're going to fire someone, it's essential to get legal counsel or direction from your human resources manager. They will make sure you have adequate documentation to justify the discharge. The last thing you want to do is hunt for documentation *after* a fired worker has sued for unlawful discharge. Why take chances?

Here is a list of do's and don'ts on firing:

Do's

1. Make sure all of your reviews are free of remarks that could be seen as prejudicial. State all complaints objectively and base them on behavior. Make sure you provide a realistic opportunity (i.e., probation) for the employee to address the reason for the termination and correct the problem.

2. Keep written documentation to show that the termination was consistent with company policy.

3. Obtain a signed, written account from the employee that gives their side of the story. If they refuse to write up and sign what they believe to have happened, that can be considered by a court as an admission of wrongdoing.

4. Make sure you have a legitimate business purpose for termination. If you do this, establish written documentation and follow procedures, you will never lose sleep over a firing.

TERMINATIONS (Continued)

Here are some "don'ts" to consider.

Don'ts

1. Procrastinate. Knowing when to fire is as important as knowing how. Failure to fire in a timely manner can do you irreparable harm. Your personal strength, commitment and ability to lead will be called into question if you don't have the guts and good judgment to fire someone who should be let go.

2. Accuse employees of vague or general complaints (i.e., poor attitude). Keep things businesslike. By implementing a program of progressive discipline, you can document and prove reasons for the termination and stay out of hot water yourself.

3. Fire on the spot. If your company policy calls for written and oral warnings, suspensions, and so on, this is one area where it is mandatory you do things by the book.

4. Discuss the firing with anyone else. Especially a potential future employer of the person fired.

What you say may be used against you by the fired employee.

SECTION VI

Some Final Thoughts

"Complexities are of our own making. Life is not complex for the person of fixed principles who has a straight course and has courage and self-control."

—Malcolm Forbes

SOME FINAL THOUGHTS

To be an effective manager, assess what you are doing in terms of responsibility, not glamour. Be more concerned with the truth of any situation than the opinions of others. Focus on getting the job done—not on earning praise or avoiding blame.

Pay attention to long-term productivity, rather than temporary ups and downs. Be as ready to accept responsibility for failure as you are to accept praise for success.

Your biggest responsibility is to confirm where you are headed with your sales team, and how you are going to help get them there. As a manger you must be concerned about strategy and execution. Your job is to achieve the goals set by you and your organization.

Charles Vest, president of Massachusetts Institute of Technology, said, ''As I look around, I fear large segments of our citizens have lost the will to excel.'' Dedicate yourself to excellence.

Einstein once said, ''Genius is simplicity.'' Return to basics as taught in this book: do it, fix it, try it. Stress fundamentals. Fundamentals of great sales managers are a constant state of awareness, devotion and commitment. Great sales managers encourage, create and maintain a climate for success.

A recent survey by *Psychology Today* of 1,700 sales managers from *Fortune* 1000 companies stated: ''Hard work coupled with results is the single most important factor in bringing about success.'' As a manager, you are judged, evaluated, promoted and valued based on your results with the people you manage.

MOVING FROM SUCCEED TO EXCEL

So far, we've concentrated mainly about how to *succeed* as a competent sales manager. Now, it is time to focus on how to *excel*.

In recruiting, extraordinary success depends largely on your ability to attract and retain the best possible sales team. This is one of your biggest challenges. Your interpersonal skills will play an increasingly important role in keeping the best people producing to the levels of their capabilities.

To distinguish yourself in recruiting, bear in mind the following:

1) Emphasize values when hiring. It is far easier to hire someone who agrees with your values than to instill a new value system.

2) Look for qualities you can't train. Jim Nordstrom of Nordstrom Department Stores, in response to a question about who trained his outstanding sales force, said, "Their parents." What he meant is that you should hire people with basic character traits such as integrity, honesty, motivation, resilience, initiative, personality and energy.

3) Constantly keep people in line to be hired and promoted. Make sure your pipeline stays full. Look inside your own organization for people with energy, enthusiasm and outstanding work records. Network constantly for exceptional people. Join professional associations.

4) Fire when necessary. You cannot recruit good people if the people you have are poisoning the environment with negativity, poor work habits or unacceptable results.

YOUR ATTITUDE CAN MOVE YOU TO GREATNESS

There are a few key attributes that characterize the truly great sales managers. Check each response to see how you are doing. Then explore how you could do these things better as indicated by your response.

	DO WELL NOW	COULD DO BETTER
1) Bias toward action. *"Things come to those who wait, but only things left by those who hustle."* —Abraham Lincoln	☐	☐
2) Simplicity. Sales is not complex. It is a matter of applied consistency.	☐	☐
3) Commitment. Being 70% committed is the same as zero. You can't be a little bit committed.	☐	☐
4) Persistence. *"No problem can stand the assault of sustained thinking."* —Voltaire	☐	☐
5) Appreciation of experience. There are no mistakes, only lessons. Each lesson is repeated until it is learned, and the overall learning process does not end.	☐	☐
6) Adjustment to circumstances. Everyone's different, so don't treat everyone alike.	☐	☐
7) Listening ability. The highest compliment you can pay to your people is to listen to what they have to say.	☐	☐

VOICE OF EXPERIENCE

If you could start out with the savvy and the experience of a seasoned sales manager, what mistakes would you avoid? These 10 errors could be avoided by new sales managers if they only knew about them in advance.

10 TIPS FOR SUCCESS

1) Be painstakingly careful when you hire.
2) Regularly ask your people their opinions.
3) Hold your people accountable for their actions.
4) Have your people make a commitment to their goals.
5) Provide autonomy for your salespeople.
6) Provide freedom for people who need it and controls for others, (i.e., understand and react to individual differences.)
7) Maintain on-going contact with your customers and markets.
8) Be honest about reality (including bad news).
9) Be straightforward in your discussions (don't keep people guessing).
10) Always look for ways to improve your skills and abilities.

REWARDS FOR TOP ACHIEVERS

"The reward of doing a thing well is having done it."
—Emerson

Most salespeople, according to B.F. Skinner's theory on positive reinforcement, perform better when they expect to get recognition or a reward. Our society is based on a reward system from childhood on, beginning with gold stars, report cards, etc.

The key to rewarding high achievers it to provide rewards that unmistakably recognize the uniqueness of their accomplishments. Top sales managers will find what works best for their team members. It can range from special gifts such as gold watches to exclusive ceremonies such as recognition dinners.

Appeal to pride and ego. Build tradition. Your superstars have the same need for recognition, validation and acceptance as those newly hired. Giving thoughtful recognition is no trifling matter. It is the very stuff that creates the environment winners need to thrive.

SELF-ASSESSMENT:

Answer these questions and notice the areas where you can improve your ability to create more superstars in your sales force. Develop a plan to convert your "no's" into "yeses."

	YES	NO
1. Do I have, in writing, a clearly defined set of sales goals?	☐	☐
2. Do I have these goals broken down into monthly increments?	☐	☐
3. Am I doing the right things today that will move me closer to my short-term goal?	☐	☐
4. Do I plan each week?	☐	☐
5. Do I plan my most important tasks for completion during my priority time?	☐	☐
6. Do I concentrate on objectives instead of procedures?	☐	☐
7. Do I judge myself on accomplishments rather than activity?	☐	☐
8. Do I set priorities according to importance rather than urgency?	☐	☐
9. Do I make constructive use of time, both in the office and in the field?	☐	☐
10. Do I delegate as much as possible?	☐	☐
11. Do I think of ways to challenge my people?	☐	☐
12. Do I grant authority along with responsibilities?	☐	☐
13. Am I open to feedback?	☐	☐
14. Do I feel in control of my responsibilities and my life?	☐	☐
15. Do I prevent unneeded intrusions on my time?	☐	☐
16. Do I keep my files organized and up-to-date?	☐	☐

SELF-ASSESSMENT (Continued)

	YES	NO
17. In communication, do I clearly state issues?	☐	☐
18. Do I summarize key points well, both verbally and in writing?	☐	☐
19. Do I make decisions promptly and with authority?	☐	☐
20. Do I assign responsibility?	☐	☐
21. Do I handle important matters in person when I have the choice?	☐	☐
22. Do I use written communication effectively—making sure that everything requiring a written response receives one?	☐	☐
23. Do I try to ensure there is balance in my life so I won't burn out on the job?	☐	☐
24. Am I constantly thinking about ways to do my job better?	☐	☐
25. Do I keep my briefcase stacked so I use "trash time" efficiently?	☐	☐
26. Do I live in the present? Am I realistic?	☐	☐
27. Do I think in terms of both what needs to be done today *and* tomorrow?	☐	☐
28. Do I strive to work in the field with every member of my sales team at least once each month?	☐	☐
29. Do I have regular goal reviews, both personal and for my employees?	☐	☐
30. Do I keep myself current through reading, training and other education?	☐	☐
31. Do I work to prepare my people for more responsibility? Have I trained a successor to myself?	☐	☐
32. Are my actions determined by me instead of by circumstances or other people's priorities?	☐	☐

DEVELOP A PERSONAL ACTION PLAN

Think over the material you read in this book. Review the self-assessment you just completed. Rethink the other exercises. What have you learned about management? What have you learned about yourself as a manager? How can you apply what you have learned to your sales team?

Make a commitment to become a more effective manager by designing a personal action plan to help you accomplish this goal. The following guide will help you clarify your goals and outline the actions you need to take to achieve them.

1. My management strengths include:

2. I need to improve my management skills in the following areas:

3. My goals for improving my management skills are as follows (be sure they are specific, attainable and measurable):

4. These are the people who can help me achieve my goals:

5. Following are my specific action steps, along with a timetable to achieve each goal:

GROWING AS A SALES MANAGER

How do you keep your attitude in tip-top shape, no matter what's going on? Maintain your passion, increase your satisfaction and meditate on your purpose.

Here are some questions to ask yourself to keep things moving in the right direction: onward and upward!

A. MAINTAIN YOUR PASSION

1. Do you basically love what you do?
2. Do you do it for your own reasons?
3. Have you become immersed in your job and your industry?
4. Do you constantly find ways to upgrade your skills?
5. Do you have fun?

B. INCREASE YOUR SATISFACTION

1. Do you seek to expand your personal experiences and horizons?
2. Do you work at finding mentors and thus learn from them?
3. Do you listen to yourself?
4. Do you read motivating, stimulating subjects?
5. Do you explore new areas and willingly accept new challenges?

C. RETHINK YOUR PURPOSE

1. How much time do you take for self-management?
2. Have you clarified your primary purpose (both personal and career)?
3. Is your life reflecting your values and priorities?
4. Do you have a personal mission statement?
5. Do you celebrate your uniqueness?

THE PERFECT SALES MANAGER

Perfect sales managers inherit, recruit and train ordinary people whom they help make extraordinary. They take diverse personalities and mold them into a solid, efficient team. They lead by personal example and always provide fresh challenges.

They never use a hard sell but are always compelling. They genuinely care for their employees and their customers. Perfect sales managers bring out the best in people.

They are positive thinkers and solution oriented. They never manipulate. Instead, they inspire and develop. Poor performance is addressed quickly, openly and directly.

It is through genuine concern of others that perfect sales managers make their biggest impact, contributing to the growth of people and the success of business.

NOTES

NOTES

NOTES

NOTES

NOTES

ISBN	Title / Author	Price Rs. 99/- Each
— 8176495867	**Managing Anger** by Rebecca Luhn Wolfe	
— 8176495891	**Managing for Commitment** by Carol Kinsey Goman	
— 8176495905	**Managing Negative People** by S. Michael Kravitz	
— 8176496960	**Partners in Performance** by Tony Moglia	
	COACHING AND MENTORING	
— 8176495166	**Be Your Own Coach** by B. Braham & C. Wahl	
— 817649531X	**Coaching and Counseling** by Marianne Minor	
— 8176495328	**Coaching for Development** by Marianne Minor	
— 8176495859	**Making the Most of Being Mentored** by Gordon F. Shea	
— 8176495999	**Mentoring** by Gordon F. Shea	
	VERBAL COMMUNICATION	
— 8176496731	**50 One-Minute Tips to Better Communication** by P. E. Bozek	
— 8176495336	**Communicating With Employees** by Frank M. Corrado	
— 8176495557	**Effective Meeting Skills** by Marion E. Haynes	
— 8176495611	**Emotional Intelligence Works** by M. Kravitz & S. D. Schubert	
— 8176495727	**Giving and Receiving Feedback** by Patti Hathaway	
— 8176495840	**Making Humor Work** by Terry Paulson	
— 8176495107	**The Art of Communicating** by Bert Decker	
— 8176495255	**The Business of Listening** by Diana Bonet	
— 817649724X	**Thinking on Your Feet** by Marlene Caroselli	
	WRITTEN COMMUNICATION	
— 8176495190	**Better Business Writing** by Susan L. Brock	
— 8176495301	**Clear Writing** by Diana Bonet	
— 8176495670	**Fat-Free Writing** by Carol Andrus	
— 8176496928	**Powerful Proofreading Skills** by D. Smith & H. Sutton	
— 8176497193	**Technical Writing in the Corporate World** by H. Estrin & N. Elliot	
— 8176495220	**The Building Blocks of Business Writing** by Jack Swenson	
— 8176497371	**Writing Business Proposals and Reports** by Susan L. Brock	
— 8176497398	**Writing Fitness** by Jack Swenson	
— 8176497401	**Writing That Sells** by Kathleen A. Begley	
	PRESENTATION SKILLS	
— 8176495581	**Effective Presentation Skills** by Steve Mandel	
— 8176497185	**Technical Presentation Skills** by Steve Mandel	
— 8176497304	**Using Visual Aids** by C. Raines & L. Williamson	

ISBN	Title / Author	Price Rs. 99/- Each
ELECTRONIC COMMUNICATION		
— 817649738X	**Writing Effective E-Mail** by Nancy Flynn	
CONFLICT RESOLUTION		
— 8176495883	**Managing Disagreement Constructively** by Herbert S. Kindler	
CUSTOMER SERVICE		
— 8176496839	**A Positive Guide to Superior Service** by William Martin	
— 8176495018	**Beyond Customer Service** by Richard F. Gerson	
— 8176496863	**Calming Upset Customers** by Rebecca Morgan	
— 8176495441	**Customer Satisfaction** by Dru Scott	
— 8176495921	**Managing Quality Customer Service** by William B. Martin	
— 8176495972	**Measuring Customer Satisfaction** by R. Gerson	
— 817649691X	**Most Customer Services Start With the Telephone** by Nancy Friedman	
TELEPHONE SKILLS		
— 8176497207	**Telephone Courtesy & Customer Service** by Lloyd C. Finch	
CALL CENTER SUCCESS		
— 8176495271	**Call Center Success** by Lloyd C. Finch	
SALES AND MARKETING		
— 8176496847	**Achieve Large-Budget Marketing Without a Large Budget** by Richard Gerson	
— 8176495204	**Building and Closing the Sale** by V. Thornton	
— 8176495263	**Business Research** by P. Timm & R. Farr	
— 8176495360	**Consultative Sales Power** by Karen Mantyla	
— 817649545X	**Dealing Effectively With the Media** by John Wade	
— 8176495514	**Direct Marketing Techniques** by Lois Geller	
— 8176495603	**Effective Sales Management** by Tom Johnson	
— 8176495964	**Marketing Your Consulting or Professional Services** by D. Karlson	
— 8176497029	**Prospecting: The Key to Sales Success** by Virden Thornton	
— 8176496774	**Sales Training Basics** by Elwood Chapman	
— 8176497339	**Winning the Inner Game of Selling** by Richard Gerson	
PRODUCTIVITY		
— 8176495085	**Achieving Results** by Lorna Riley	
— 8176495093	**Administrative Assistant** by Brenda Bailey-Hughes	
— 8176496820	**Plan Your Work: Work Your Plan** by James Sherman	
— 8176497134	**Successful Self-Management** by Paul R. Timm	

ISBN	Title / Author	Price Rs. 99/- Each
	TIME MANAGEMENT	
— 817649674X	**Office Management** by M. Manning & P. Haddock	
— 8176496766	**Personal Time Management** by Marion E. Haynes	
— 8176497010	**Professionalism in the Office** by Marilyn Manning	
— 8176497231	**The Telephone and Time Management** by Dru Scott	
	SELF IMPROVEMENT	
— 8176495077	**Achieving Job Satisfaction** by Editors of Crisp Publications, Inc	
— 8176495123	**Attitude** by E. Chapman & W. Mcknight	
— 8176495298	**Clear and Creative Thinking** by Herb Kindler	
— 8176495344	**Concentration** by Sam Horn	
— 8176495433	**Critical Thinking** by Daniel A. Feldman	
— 8176495492	**Developing Positive Assertiveness** by Sam R. Lloyd	
— 8176495506	**Developing Self-Esteem** by Connie Palladino	
— 8176495646	**Ethics in Business** by R. Maddux & D. Maddux	
— 817649688X	**Finding Your Purpose** by Barbara J. Braham	
— 8176495980	**Memory Skills in Business** by Madelyn Burley-Allen	
— 8176497061	**Risk Taking** by Herbert Kindler	
	JOBS AND CAREERS	
— 817649528X	**Career Discovery Program** by Elwood N. Chapman	
— 8176495409	**Creating Your Skills Portfolio** by Carrie Straub	
— 8176495565	**Effective Networking** by Venda Raye-Johnson	
— 8176495719	**Getting Hired** by Richard Pinsker	
— 8176494569	**Networking for Success** by Nancy Flynn	
— 8176496944	**Preparing for the Behavior-Based Interview** by T. Fitzwater	
— 8176497002	**Preparing for Your Interview** by Diane Berk	
— 8176497088	**Strategic Resumes** by Marci Mahoney	
— 817649741X	**Your First Thirty Days** by E. Chapman & R. Maddux	
	PEER RELATIONS & APPEARANCE	
— 8176495247	**Business Etiquette & Professionalism** by M. Kay duPont	
— 817649576X	**Improving Peer Relationships** by Norman Hill	
— 8176495786	**Influence** by Elaina Zuker	
— 8176495794	**Influencing Others** by William Nothstine	
— 8176495956	**Managing Upward** by Patti Hathaway	
— 8176496936	**Office Politics** by Rebecca Luhn Wolfe	

	ISBN	Title / Author	Price Rs. 99/- Each
—	8176496979	**Personal Counseling** by R. Knowdell & E. Chapman	
—	8176494593	**Winning at Human Relations** by Elwood N. Chapman	
		ADULT LEARNING	
—	8176495131	**Basic Business Math** by Richard P. Truchon	
—	8176495697	**Formatting Letters and Reports** by Eleanor Davidson	
—	8176496901	**Improve Your Reading Improve Your Job** by Jeanne Miller	
—	817649710X	**Study Skills Strategies** by Uelaine Lengefeld	
—	8176497118	**Successful Life Long Learning** by Robert Steinbach	
—	8176497320	**Vocabulary Improvement** by Diana Bonet	
		CREATIVITY	
—	8176495417	**Creative Decision Making** by H. B. Gelatt	
—	8176495425	**Creativity in Business** by Carol Kinsey Goman	
		STRESS, WELL-BEING & RETIREMENT	
—	817649593X	**Managing Stress for Mental Fitness** by M. Raber & G. Dyck	
—	8176497096	**Stress that Stress That Motivates** by Dru Scott	
		COMPLIANCE	
—	8176495522	**Disaster Preparedness** by J. Freestone & R. Raab	
		HIRING AND MANAGING	
—	817649500X	**50 One-Minute Tips for Recruiting Employees** by Hayes & Ninemeier	
—	8176494526	**50 One-Minute Tips for Retaining Employees** by Hayes & NInemeier	
—	8176495034	**About Pay** by James F. Carey	
—	8176495115	**Attacking Absenteeism** by Lynn Tylczak	
—	8176495174	**Behavior-Based Interviewing** by Terry Fitzwater	
—	817649559X	**Effective Recruiting Strategies** by R. Visconti & M. Brounstein	
—	817649562X	**Employee Suggestion Systems** by C. Martin & R. Bassford	
—	8176495751	**High Performance Hiring** by Robert Wendover	
—	8176496995	**Personnel Testing** by John Jones	
—	8176497037	**Quality Interviewing** by Robert Maddux	
—	8176497045	**Recruiting for High Performance** by Robert Wendover	
—	8176497363	**Writing a Human Resources Manual** by S. Brock & S. Cabbell	
		TRAINING	
—	8176495026	**50 One-Minute Tips for Trainers** by Carrie Van Daele	
—	8176495352	**Conducting a Needs Analysis** by Geri McArdle	
—	8176495476	**Delivering Effective Training Sessions** by Geri McArdle	

	ISBN	Title / Author Price Rs. 99/- Each
—	8176495484	**Developing Instructional Design** by Geri McArdle
—	8176495549	**Dynamics of Diversity** by Odette Pollar
—	8176496898	**Graphics for Presenters** by Lynn Kearny
—	8176497266	**Training Managers to Train** by David Hayes
—	8176497274	**Training Methods That Work** by Lois Hart
—	8176497355	**Working Together** by George Simons
		STRATEGIC DEVELOPMENT
—	8176496871	**Competency and the Learning Organization** by Donald Shandler
—	8176495395	**Creating a Learning Organization** by Barbara Braham
—	8176496758	**Organization Development** by Lenny Ralphs
—	8176496952	**Organizational Vision, Values and Mission** by Scott, Jaffe & Tobe
—	8176497142	**Successful Strategic Planning** by Stephen Haines
—	8176497169	**Systematic Succession Planning** by Rebecca Wolfe
—	8176494585	**Understanding Leadership Competencies** by Guggenheimer & Szulc
		FINANCE
—	8176495050	**The Accounting Cycle** by J. Jacquet & W. Miller
—	8176495855	**Basics of Budgeting** by Terry Dickey
—	8176495689	**Financial Analysis** by J. Gill & M. Chatton
—	8176496987	**Personal Financial Fitness** by Allen Klosowski
—	817649707X	**Starting Your New Business** by Charles Martin
—	8176497290	**Understanding Financial Statements** by James Gill
		CHANGE
—	8176495387	**Coping With Workplace Change** by J. Jeffreys
—	8176495875	**Managing Change at Work** by C. Scott & D. Jaffe
—	8176495913	**Managing Personal Change** by C. Scott & Dennis Jaffe
—	8176497282	**Understanding Organizational Change** by L. Fossum
		MANUFACTURING AND INVENTORY
—	817649514X	**Basics of Inventory Management** by J. Viale
—	8176495158	**Basics of Manufacturing** by J. Viale
—	8176495182	**Benchmarking Basics** by James Patterson
—	8176495212	**Building a Total Quality Culture** by Joe Batten
—	8176495816	**JIT Forecasting and Master Scheduling** by J. Viale
—	8176495379	**The Continuously Improving Self** by J. Lickson
—	8176497258	**TQM** by JoAnn Haberer & M. Webb

Prices are subject to change without notice.